INSPIRING

OLYMPIC

STORIES

FOR

YOUNG READERS

CONTENTS

Introduction

Ever dreamt of reaching the top? The athletes in this book have - all the way to the Olympics! But their journeys weren't smooth. They faced doubts and setbacks, just like you might during a tough test or mastering a new skill.

Here's the secret they discovered: those wobbly moments don't have to stop you. Remember that time you aced something even after a few bumps? That's perseverance!

This book introduces you to inspiring young people who overcome challenges, discover their strength, and achieve their dreams. You'll learn that believing in yourself and giving your all are the keys to unlocking your own potential.

Get ready to be inspired! Grab your backpack of determination and climb your own personal mountain!

Simone Biles: A Star Who Redefined Greatness

Simone Biles wasn't born to be ordinary. Her energy crackled through the Biles household in Columbus, Ohio. Her parents, Ron and Nellie, nicknamed her "Little Hurricane" for a reason. From the moment she could walk, she was a whirlwind of motion, climbing furniture, cartwheeling down hallways, and turning grocery store aisles into impromptu balance beams.

School was a struggle. Sitting still wasn't in Simone's DNA. Nellie, a nurse, noticed the frustration brewing in her daughter. "Simone needed an outlet, a release for that boundless energy," she later recalled. One afternoon, while flipping through a magazine, Nellie stumbled upon an ad for a local gymnastics academy. A seed was planted.

Simone's first foray into gymnastics wasn't exactly graceful. At six years old, she was a little on the stocky side compared to the other girls, her limbs seemingly thicker and less flexible. But what she lacked in classical form, she made up for in raw power and an infectious enthusiasm. Coach Aimee Boorman saw a spark in Simone, a determination that shone brighter than any physical limitation.

Simone took to gymnastics like a duck to water. She soaked up instructions, her body translating them into gravity-defying feats. Her flips had a unique power, a dynamism that set her apart. Even her smile, wide and unreserved, was a rebellion against the usual stoic demeanor of elite gymnasts. Simone wasn't here to fit in; she was here to redefine the sport.

Simone's progress was meteoric. Within a few years, she was dominating regional competitions, her routines a mesmerizing blend of strength, agility, and sheer audacity. Her coaches, Aimee and Laurent Landi, nurtured her talent while encouraging her playful spirit. They knew that Simone's joy was a key ingredient in her success.

National recognition soon followed. By the time she was 16, Simone had captured hearts and trophies with equal ease. Her signature moves, defying established gymnastic boundaries, became known as "The Biles." "The Amanar," a daring vault named after her, sent shivers down judges' spines. Yet, Simone herself remained grounded. She aced interviews, her bubbly personality a refreshing contrast to the usual athlete stoicism.

The 2016 Rio Olympics were the culmination of years of dedication. The pressure was immense, but Simone thrived on it. Her confidence was infectious, her smile radiating across the entire stadium. She led a squad of talented young women, aptly named the "Final Five," to a historic team gold. Individual gold medals followed, each routine a testament to her mastery of the sport.

Simone returned home a global icon. She graced magazine covers, landed lucrative sponsorships, and inspired a generation of young girls to defy expectations. She made gymnastics seem fun, a joyful dance with gravity rather than a grueling test of physical prowess.

But even the brightest stars face challenges.

The 2020 Tokyo Olympics were shrouded in uncertainty due to the pandemic. The weight of expectation, the constant training, and the isolation took their toll on Simone. She began experiencing the "twisties," a terrifying phenomenon where gymnasts lose their spatial awareness mid-air.

In a move that shocked the world, Simone prioritized her mental healthA wave of reactions followed, some praising her bravery for opening up about mental health in a sport that often ignored it. Others, however, questioned her commitment, her loyalty to her team.

But Simone didn't waver. She used her platform to shed light on the struggles of athletes, the immense pressure they experience, and the importance of prioritizing mental well-being. In doing so, she redefined strength. It wasn't just about flawless routines and gold medals; it was about courage, vulnerability, and self-care.

The decision wasn't easy. Simone, the champion known for her infectious smile, grappled with anxiety and self-doubt. But she returned to the balance beam, determined to compete on her own terms. Her bronze medal wasn't the gold everyone expected, but it symbolized something far more significant - her resilience, her self-awareness, and her victory over fear.

Today, Simone Biles stands at the crossroads. Paris 2024 beckons, but there's a newfound balance in her approach. She's an advocate for mental health, a businesswoman with her own brand, and a student at UCLA, determined to expand her horizons beyond the gym. Simone Biles is no longer just a gymnast; she's a multi-faceted role model for young people around the world.

Her decision to prioritize mental health in Tokyo sparked a global conversation. Athletes, celebrities, and everyday people alike began openly discussing the challenges they faced. Simone's vulnerability empowered others to do the same, chipping away at the stigma surrounding mental health.

This newfound focus on well-being extends to Simone's training. While her dedication remains unwavering, there's a shift towards a more sustainable approach. She prioritizes rest and recovery, listens to her body, and embraces a training environment that fosters joy alongside excellence.

The road to Paris 2024 is still unfolding. Will Simone compete? Will she add to her already staggering medal collection? These are questions only time can answer. But one thing is certain: Simone Biles has already cemented her legacy.

She's not just a gymnast who defied expectations with her revolutionary moves and infectious smile. She's a champion for mental health, a role model for young women, and a testament to the power of resilience and self-belief. Simone Biles has redefined greatness not just in gymnastics, but in the way we approach life's challenges, both on and off the competition floor.

Eric Moussambani: From Novice to Legend

Okay, let's be real: the 2000 Sydney Olympics might have been packed with star athletes, but the one name everyone remembers is Eric Moussambani. No fancy medals, no record-breaking times. This guy became a legend for being spectacularly bad. But his story is less about swimming terribly, and more about having the guts to even jump in the pool in the first place.

Eric was from Equatorial Guinea, a tiny country tucked along the African coast. Olympic-sized swimming pool? Never seen one. Ocean? Sure, he could swim a little, but mostly doggy-paddle style to avoid the sharks. So, imagine his surprise when he gets this wildcard invite to the Olympics – as a swimmer. Dude had about eight months to prepare.

News flash: eight months is NOT enough time to turn yourself into Michael Phelps if you've spent most of your life splashing about in a

12-meter hotel pool. But Eric, bless his heart, was determined. He found a coach who probably felt a mix of horror and pity, and started training at five in the morning, the only time he could use the pool before the guests woke up.

Think of it: early morning workouts, no fancy equipment, just raw determination and a whole lot of awkward thrashing around trying to mimic what he'd seen on TV. He must have looked like a fish trying to run a marathon. But Eric kept at it, day after day.

Now, let's fast-forward to Sydney. Eric arrives at this massive Olympic complex, probably feeling like a fish dropped in the Sahara. Athletes sculpted like statues, coaches barking instructions, the whole atmosphere buzzing with high-performance energy. Eric probably wondered if he'd accidentally walked onto the set of a superhero movie.

Then comes the 100-meter freestyle heats. Eric steps onto the block, the crowd buzzing, cameras flashing... and his two competitors get disqualified for false starts. Awkward. Now, most people would feel a surge of relief. But Eric? I bet he had a split-second of "Oh crap, now it's just me."

Suddenly it's a solo act, all eyes on him. You gotta admire the guy's spirit at this point. He could've pulled out with a sudden "injury" or tripped "accidentally" before the starting signal, but no. Eric takes a deep breath and dives in.

The first 50 meters actually weren't terrible. He had a kind of lumpy, frantic freestyle going on, head bobbing above water like he was scanning for those sharks. But then, the lack of actual swimming experience hit him like a ton of bricks. He started slowing down, arms flailing more than propelling, and that gasp for air every other stroke... let's just say it wasn't pretty.

The crowd went from a polite hum to full-on cheering. This wasn't about winning anymore, this was pure human spirit. They roared as Eric, doing a very interesting mix of freestyle and doggy paddle, inched closer to the finish line. The lifeguards were probably hovering close, ready to fish him out if needed.

When he finally, miraculously, touched the wall, the place exploded. His time? The slowest in Olympic history by a landslide. But you know what? Nobody cared. Eric

Moussambani, a guy who barely knew how to swim a year ago, had just completed an Olympic race. He climbed out of the pool, grinning ear to ear, and accidentally became an Olympic icon.

The media, of course, went crazy. "Eric the Eel" they nicknamed him, with a mix of affection and a dash of mockery. Some snarky articles might have hinted he was a joke, that the Olympics were losing their touch by letting someone like him participate.

But here's the thing: they all missed the point. Eric Moussambani wasn't the world's best swimmer, but he WAS the world's bravest. He dared to step way outside his comfort zone, to try something utterly absurd, and to somehow keep smiling through the chaos.

How many of us would have that kind of courage? To risk potential embarrassment on a global scale, simply for the chance to go for it. Eric, in his own hilariously unconventional way, epitomized the Olympic spirit. It's not always about the gold medal, it's about the audacity to try.

He wasn't just the underdog, he was the

"under-fish". Everyone loves a good "zero to hero" story, but Eric flipped the script. He was already kind of a low-key hero just for showing up. It gave regular people hope: if Eric could do this, maybe they could tackle that impossible thing they'd been putting off.

But Eric's story doesn't end with a viral video and a few laughs. The attention suddenly thrust upon him was a double-edged sword. Sure, there were funny TV interviews, some offers for product endorsements, a kind of goofy celebrity status.

But imagine being Eric in the whirlwind that followed. One moment you're training in a hotel pool, the next you're fielding interview requests on CNN. Fame can be intoxicating, and it takes a strong person to keep their head above water when swept away by that current.

Luckily, Eric seemed to handle it with a good dose of humor and humility. He didn't get swept up in delusions of grandeur, but he smartly seized the opportunities that came his way. With the extra attention, he got better training facilities and experienced coaching.

And here's the thing people often forget: Eric got better. A lot better. He never morphed into a swimming superstar, but he competed in several more events, shaved massive chunks off his initial time, and most importantly, became a genuinely competent swimmer. This wasn't just a 15-minutes-of-fame fluke; he put in the work.

Meanwhile, Eric became an ambassador for his country, putting Equatorial Guinea on the map in a way championships and diplomatic visits never had. He inspired young people back home, gave talks about the importance of sports, and helped raise funds to build new swimming pools – creating opportunities he never had as a kid.

There's a lesson there, beyond even the tale of the underdog. It's easy to get cynical about sudden fame, to assume it's all shallow and fleeting. But Eric's story shows how, when channeled the right way, even the most unusual platform can be turned into something lasting and meaningful.

Would his story be as memorable if he'd won a medal in Sydney? Maybe not. Sometimes, the struggles are what make the triumphs so resonant. Eric the Eel, with his awkward strokes and unbreakable determination, reminds us that there's glory even in the attempt. That sometimes, daring to splash clumsily in the deep end is its own kind of victory.

And let's be honest, if you're at a party, and someone asks "So, did you ever compete in the Olympics?" which story sounds better: "Yeah, I got a bronze in the medley," or "Well, I was kinda slow, but they called me Eric the Eel, and it was AWESOME."

Eric's tale is funny, heartwarming, and strangely profound all at once. It's about courage, the absurdity of life, and the fact that if you can laugh at yourself while giving something your all, you're already a winner in a way that really matters.

Jesse Owens: The Speed That Defied Hitler

Here's the story of Jesse Owens, an athletic icon who defied expectations and made history under the most challenging circumstances:

James Cleveland Owens wasn't born an Olympic legend. He was born in Alabama, the grandson of slaves, in a time when the color of his skin dictated more limitations than opportunities. Nicknamed "J.C." by his family, he was a skinny, sickly kid, not the picture of an athletic prodigy.

But J.C. had something special – raw, untapped speed. When his family moved to Cleveland, Ohio, seeking better chances, that speed got noticed. A middle school gym teacher with a keen eye saw potential in the lanky kid who seemed to fly across the playground. With proper training, this kid could be something extraordinary.

Owens was given his legendary name by

accident – when his thick southern accent made "J.C." sound like "Jesse" to his new teacher, the name stuck. Under the guidance of Coach Charles Riley, Jesse started to shine. He wasn't just fast – he had grace, a natural ease of motion that made him seem unstoppable. While other kids huffed and puffed, Jesse made running look effortless. Soon, he was smashing school records and turning heads.

By high school, the kid they called "The Buckeye Bullet" (a nod to his Ohio roots) was a force to be reckoned with. Jesse wasn't just winning local races; he was making national headlines. In a single record-breaking day in 1935, he tied a world record in the 100-yard dash and broke three others in long jump, 220-yard dash, and 220-yard hurdles. Imagine the internet breaking if that happened today!

The following year, Jesse Owens had his sights set on the grandest stage of all: the 1936 Olympic Games in Berlin, Germany. Problem was, at the time, Germany wasn't the most welcoming place for a Black athlete. The Nazi party, led by the infamous Adolf Hitler, had this whole warped idea about racial superiority. They believed Jesse, and athletes like him, were somehow inferior based on nothing but the color of their skin.

There was even a lot of debate about whether Jesse should go at all. Many urged him to boycott the games to protest the racist regime. But Jesse had a different plan. He was going to Berlin, not just to compete, but to dominate. He would win, and his victories would be a powerful message, a flying leap over the monstrous hate of the Nazis.

Berlin, 1936. The Olympic stadium rumbled with anticipation, and a whole lot of Nazi arrogance. But Jesse Owens wasn't intimidated. With the world watching, he stepped onto the track, the weight of history on his shoulders. Race after race, he proved the absurdity of the Nazi ideology. Jesse Owens wasn't just an athlete; he was a force of nature rewriting the rules.

He blazed to victory in the 100-meter dash. Then, he soared to a gold medal in the long jump, reportedly getting some secret advice from his German competitor (who later became his friend). The crowd, at first hesitant to cheer for a Black athlete, went wild. The Nazi officials in the stands? Not so happy. Hitler, supposedly, was absolutely fuming.

Jesse wasn't done yet. He sprinted to another gold medal in the 200-meter dash and secured a fourth (yes, a fourth!) in the 4x100 meter relay. The 1936 Berlin Olympics will forever be remembered as the time Jesse Owens single-handedly dismantled the myth of Aryan superiority. He didn't just make history; he changed it.

Sadly, even after conquering the world stage, Jesse Owens faced discrimination back home in the United States. But his legacy became a weapon in the fight for racial equality, inspiring generations of athletes and activists. He defied the odds, defied the haters, and showed the world that determination and talent can triumph over the ugliest of prejudices.

Jesse Owens' story isn't just about running or jumping. It's about the power of the human spirit to soar above injustice. He didn't just win medals; he won hearts and minds. His victories echoed far beyond the track, becoming a symbol of hope and resilience in the face of oppression. And that, maybe, is the greatest victory of them all.

Steven Bradbury: The Accidental Champion

In the world of Olympic athletes, Steven Bradbury was an oddity. An Australian ice speed skater? That was like expecting a kangaroo to win a downhill skiing competition. He wasn't young and streamlined like most of his competitors, but a bit older, with a build more suited to rugby than gliding across the ice at terrifying speeds.

His Olympic journey wasn't defined by medals, but by unfortunate encounters with both bad luck and sharp objects. His first Olympics in 1994 ended with a dramatic crash— another skater collided with him, the blade slicing through Bradbury's thigh like a knife through butter. He required 111 stitches and lost so much blood he nearly died. Yet, somehow, Bradbury got himself back on the ice.

Dedication? Stubbornness? A hint of madness? Probably a mix of all three. Four years later, disaster struck again. During training, he crashed and broke his neck.

Most sane people would've hung up their skates for good, but Bradbury spent months in a neck brace, then returned, crazier than ever.

His sheer determination had an element of absurdity that was hard not to admire...or laugh at a little.

Fast forward to the 2002 Salt Lake City Winter Olympics. Through a combination of resilience, grit, and more than a bit of dumb luck, Bradbury made it to the finals of the 1000-meter short track speed skating event. Short track is the demolition derby of ice sports. Skaters whip around the tiny rink in a blur, jockeying for position, their razor-sharp blades itching for a chance to trip up an opponent. Crashes are so common, they're practically part of the sport.

Bradbury, ever the realist, knew he was outmatched. His strategy wasn't so much about winning, as about not ending up in the hospital. He hung at the back of the pack, figuring he'd let the speed demons battle it out, and if he happened to cross the finish line without being maimed, that would be a bonus.

The quarterfinals were a fluke. Two skaters collided spectacularly right in front of him, and Bradbury, plodding along, cruised into the lead with a bewildered look on his face. The semifinals? Another crash gifted him a spot in the finals. The guy was becoming a walking good luck charm for every other skater's misfortune.

By the finals, Bradbury was facing the best of the best: Apolo Ohno, the American superstar, Li Jiajun, the reigning world champion...and good old Steven, trying his best to look like he belonged there. The starting gun fired, the others shot off like rockets, and Bradbury chugged along at the back, the picture of bewildered determination.

Here's where things transcend sports and become pure slapstick comedy. With one lap left, the leaders were in a ferocious battle for gold. Suddenly, in a scene reminiscent of a badly choreographed action movie, they all tangled, careened into the sidewall, and ended up in a glorious pile of spandex, skates, and shattered dreams.

Bradbury, in the meantime, was so far

behind the drama that he skated past the wreckage, his mouth hanging open in a mixture of shock and amusement. The crowd, stunned for a moment, erupted in a chaotic mix of laughter and cheers. Bradbury, realizing he was somehow the only one left standing, crossed the finish line looking like a man who'd just won a very unexpected raffle.

He hadn't earned that gold medal with blinding speed or masterful technique. Fate, it seemed, had tripped up everyone else and dropped the prize in his lap. The media went wild. "The Accidental Hero," they called him. "The Lottery Winner." Bradbury, a true Aussie bloke, handled his newfound fame with good-natured humor. Sure, it wasn't how he'd imagined Olympic glory, but hey, he'd take it.

Steven Bradbury became a legend not because he was the best, but because he embodied the absurdity and unpredictability of life itself. "Doing a Bradbury" became Australian slang for a fluke success.

He taught the world that sometimes, the most unlikely victories are the sweetest, that perseverance comes in many forms, and if you hang around long enough, absolutely anything can happen. Even a slightly bewildered Aussie with more luck than common sense can become a champion.

Usain Bolt: The Lightning Bolt Who Rocked the Track

Little Usain Bolt was a hurricane disguised as a child. Energy crackled around him like static electricity, and his preferred mode of transportation wasn't walking – it was sprinting. Now, this wasn't fueled by Olympic dreams or a burning desire for athletic glory. Usain simply hated chores. Helping his momma, Jennifer, around the house was a fate worse than facing a hungry lion (well, maybe not that bad, but close!).

His escapes involved a generous dose of mischief and a whole lot of speed. He'd outrun grumpy cows with surprising ferocity (seriously, those things can be terrifying!), leave frustrated teachers in his dust when homework duty slipped his mind (which happened... often), and occasionally, when the stars aligned, participate in track meets. But even then, the real motivation usually resided at the finish line – snacks.

Jamaica, Usain's island home, was a place

where sports, particularly running, flowed through people's veins. Usain possessed raw talent, naturally. His long legs devoured the ground with each stride, leaving other kids gasping in his wake. But focus? That was a word used more in scolding than celebration. Training sessions felt like an eternity, coaches droned on about technique, and honestly, lounging on the beach with a good jerk chicken sandwich sounded infinitely more appealing.

His first real taste of victory arrived courtesy of a classic motivator: food. The prize for winning a local race was lunch, and suddenly, Usain became the picture of dedication. Turns out, he loved the thrill of the win even more than he loved fried chicken (which, for Usain, was saying something!). Something clicked within him. There was a rush that transcended outrunning cows – the pure exhilaration of being the fastest, of pushing his limits and crossing the finish line first.

Even as a teenager, Usain wasn't your average, stoic athlete. He was a showman, a human firework waiting to explode with energy. He'd high-five the crowd before races, break into victory dances that might have made Michael Jackson jealous, and radiate pure joy while leaving everyone else in his proverbial dust.

The serious running world wasn't sure what to make of him. Was he arrogant? Disrespectful to the sport? Or was he a breath of fresh air in a world that sometimes took itself a little too seriously? One thing was certain – you couldn't ignore him.

The 2008 Beijing Olympics were his grand unveiling, his coming-out party on the world stage. And it wasn't just about winning; it was how he won. In the highly anticipated 100-meter final, the most watched race on the planet, he shattered the world record so dramatically that it seemed like a glitch in the Matrix. He even had the audacity to slow down and celebrate before he crossed the finish line!

People lost their minds. The image of "Lightning Bolt" (his self-proclaimed nickname, naturally) striking his iconic victory pose became etched in sporting history. Usain wasn't just fast; he was electrifying. He brought personality and a joyful swagger to a sport that often felt focused on grimacing and grueling training.

Over the next few Olympics, Usain cemented his legend. He collected gold medals like trophies, each victory more thrilling than the last. He broke his own "unbreakable" records, not by a hair's breadth, but by margins that left the competition utterly demoralized. It was as if everyone else was running in slow motion while Usain existed on a different plane of speed.

Usain Bolt transcended the image of a typical athlete. He was an Olympic superstar, a meme machine, the guy everyone wanted to be best friends with. But refreshingly, for someone of his fame, he remained down-to-earth.

He was obsessed with chicken nuggets (same, Usain, same). He loved to dance, even if his moves were more enthusiastic than graceful. He trained hard, but also understood the importance of balance and living life to the fullest. This made him both aspirational and relatable. He showed the world that you could be the absolute best at something and still have a blast doing it.

Behind the scenes, there was a different side to Usain. He was a dedicated athlete who respected the sport, even if his path to greatness wasn't always conventional. He gave back to his Jamaican community, a constant source of pride for him. He supported other young athletes, both financially and with motivational words. He wasn't afraid to speak out on issues he cared about, using his platform to advocate for social change.

Injuries, as they do with all athletes, eventually slowed Usain down. His retirement left a void in the sport – no one quite filled his shoes (although some are getting closer!). But his legacy extends far beyond medals and records.

Yusra Mardini: The Swim of Survival

Get ready for the story of Yusra Mardini – a Syrian swimmer whose Olympic dreams led her on a journey far more dangerous and inspiring than anyone could have imagined.

Yusra Mardini wasn't born a hero; she was born a swimmer. She grew up in Syria, and the pool was her happy place, where the chaos of the world faded away with each stroke. Her dad, a swim coach, saw her potential, and together they dreamed of the Olympics.

But Syria wasn't the safest place for dreams. The civil war was getting worse. Bombs could fall anytime, turning ordinary days into a fight for survival. Training was often impossible – the pool might be damaged, or the roads too dangerous to travel. Yet, Yusra had a stubborn kind of hope. Even as her country crumbled, she clung to her Olympic dream.

Then came the day that changed everything. Their house was destroyed.

Staying in Syria was no longer an option. It was time to escape. Imagine being crammed onto a tiny, overloaded inflatable boat with 20 other desperate people, crossing the sea for a chance at a new life. That was Yusra's reality, along with her sister Sarah. Their journey from Syria to Europe was treacherous, a gamble against the odds.

Then, the unthinkable happened. The boat's motor died in the middle of the Aegean Sea. It started to sink, the flimsy rubber no match for the waves. Passengers panicked, their meager belongings thrown overboard to lighten the load. Yusra looked at her sister, both talented swimmers. They knew what they had to do.

Yusra, Sarah, and one other man jumped into the freezing water. For over three grueling hours, they swam, kicking and pulling the sinking boat toward a distant shore. Their muscles burned, hypothermia set in, but the fear of drowning, of losing everything, was a stronger force. Because of them, everyone on board reached Europe alive.

Just let that sink in: she trained her whole life for the Olympics, and in a cruel twist of fate, the skills that were supposed to earn her medals instead saved her life.

Yusra eventually made it to Germany, gaining refugee status. Could she still dream of the Olympics? It seemed like madness. She'd lost her home, endured unimaginable trauma, and now, she was a stranger in a strange land.

But Yusra had an athlete's determination, and a sliver of hope still flickered within her. She found a swim club in Berlin and started training again. Slowly, the joy returned to her swimming, the simple rhythm of the strokes a balm for her wounded spirit.

The International Olympic Committee took notice. They formed the Refugee Olympic Team – a small group of athletes displaced from their countries due to war or persecution. Yusra was selected. Suddenly, the Olympics were possible again, but in a way she never could have imagined.

In the 2016 Rio Olympics, Yusra wasn't competing for medals; she was competing for something larger. She raced in the 100m butterfly, representing the millions of refugees worldwide. She didn't win her heat, but the moment she dove into that Olympic pool, she'd already claimed a victory far more profound.

Yusra Mardini became a beacon of hope, not just for refugees, but for anyone facing impossible odds. Here was proof of the incredible strength within the human spirit. She went on to become a Goodwill Ambassador, traveling the world and using her voice to advocate for those who've been forced to flee their homes.

Her story doesn't end with Olympic races. It's a story still being written, filled with challenges, setbacks, and the unwavering belief that even when life throws you into the stormy sea, you can swim your way towards the shore. Yusra Mardini isn't just an athlete; she's a reminder that true heroes aren't always found on a podium. Sometimes, they're found in the most unexpected places, pushing against the current with unyielding determination.

Jamaican Bobsled Team: From Sun to Snow

Imagine a bobsleigh team. Picture sleek crafts speeding down icy tracks, piloted by bundled-up athletes who brave bone-chilling winds. Now, picture that same scene, but replace the snow with palm trees and the athletes with guys in shorts. That's the crazy story of the Jamaican Bobsled Team, a group of determined dudes who defied the odds and became sporting legends.

It all started in the 1980s with a Jamaican army officer named George Fitch. Jamaica, a beautiful island nation known for its beaches and reggae music, doesn't exactly scream "winter wonderland." Yet, George stumbled upon the idea of a Jamaican bobsleigh team. Talk about an underdog story waiting to happen!

George, along with his buddy Dudley Stokes, knew nothing about bobsleigh. They'd never even seen snow, let alone raced down a mountain on ice in a tiny metal rocket. But they had something even more powerful – pure, unadulterated determination.

Their journey to the Olympics was like pushing a fridge uphill through molasses. They had zero experience, limited funding, and a complete lack of proper equipment. Imagine trying to practice bobsled runs in tropical heat by pushing a car on regular pavement! Talk about a recipe for disaster (and some serious sweat).

News of these ambitious Jamaicans spread like wildfire. The world couldn't help but be charmed by their underdog spirit. Soon, they were getting a helping hand from unexpected places. A businessman donated a second-hand bobsled they affectionately nicknamed "Sanka." (Think beat-up car with rusty wheels, but way, way colder.)

Through relentless training (and a few spectacular crashes – let's be honest, learning bobsleigh on the fly is a recipe for some bumps and bruises!), the team secured a spot in the 1988 Winter Olympics in Calgary, Canada. Talk about a culture clash! From sunny beaches to snowy mountains, these guys were about to experience a winter wonderland unlike anything they'd ever imagined.

The Calgary Olympics were a spectacle. The Jamaican team, with their infectious enthusiasm and bright smiles, became instant crowd favorites. Sure, the other teams were seasoned veterans with fancy equipment and years of experience. But the Jamaicans had something they couldn't buy – heart.

The actual race was...well, eventful. Remember that beat-up bobsled named Sanka? It wasn't exactly built for Olympic speeds. During one run, a steering bolt sheared off, sending the Jamaicans on a wild, out-of-control ride down the track. Miraculously, they all emerged unharmed, though a little shaken (and probably with a newfound respect for proper equipment).

Despite the crash, the Jamaicans didn't finish last. More importantly, they didn't give up. They finished the race with a smile, earning the respect and admiration of the entire world. They may not have gotten a medal, but they won something far more valuable – the hearts of millions.

The story of the Jamaican Bobsled Team became a symbol of determination, perseverance, and the power of believing in the impossible. It even inspired a hilarious movie called "Cool Runnings," which made their story even more famous.

The Jamaican Bobsled Team's legacy goes beyond their Olympic run. They showed the world that passion and hard work can take you places you never thought possible, even if you have to start with a rusty fridge on wheels and zero experience.

So, the next time you feel like giving up on a dream, remember the Jamaican Bobsled Team. They slid headfirst into a crazy challenge and proved that sometimes, the most epic journeys start with the most unexpected ideas.

Wilma Rudolph: From Polio to Olympic Champion.

Wilma Rudolph wasn't born to be an athlete. She was born tiny, sickly, her left leg twisted and weak from a bout of childhood polio. The braces and corrective shoes were her constant companions, and doctors said with grim certainty that she'd never walk normally, let alone run.

But Wilma had a fire burning in her that crutches and diagnoses couldn't extinguish. She came from a big, boisterous family in Tennessee – twenty-two kids in total, and not a single one of them would pity her. When her brothers and sisters bolted outside to play, Wilma gritted her teeth and followed, hobbling and determined. If they played tag, they weren't about to go easy on her. She fell, got back up, fell again, and eventually, she started to fall a little less often.

Those early games in the dusty yard weren't about athletic glory, they were about defiance. She refused to be left on the sidelines, to be defined by what her body couldn't do. It hurt, both physically and in the sting of a prideful child's heart, but with every stubborn step, Wilma was building a kind of strength that had nothing to do with muscles.

Then came the day her momma announced it was time for the brace to come off. The doctor had agreed – Wilma's leg had healed as much as it was going to. She stood there, thin legs wobbling, and with a mix of terror and hope, took her first unassisted steps. It was awkward, clumsy, and her mama had to catch her a few times, but she was *walking*.

Walking wasn't enough for Wilma. She wanted to run, the way her siblings did, with the freedom and joy of a body in full flight. Her family became her training team. They teased her relentlessly, challenging her to races, playing basketball where no one would take it easy on 'the cripple' as some kids had cruelly called her.

Those backyard competitions lit a competitive spark in Wilma. She discovered that she was fast, maybe not as effortlessly as her siblings, but with enough determination, she could leave them in the dust.

There's no understating the power of a single person who believes in you when you barely believe in yourself. For Wilma, that person was Ed Temple, her high school track coach. When Coach Temple first saw Wilma, all skinny arms and legs, he wasn't thinking "future Olympian." But she had heart, and he recognized that raw, unbreakable spirit.

At first, she could barely finish a practice. Those years of walking unevenly had taken their toll, and the muscles that should have carried her smoothly forward were a tangled, protesting mess. Coach Temple didn't sugarcoat it – the road ahead would be tough, full of both sweat and tears.

That's the funny thing about a challenge – for the right kind of person, it's like fuel instead of a deterrent. Wilma nicknamed herself "the flightless bird," both self-deprecating and strangely accurate. But she put in the grueling hours. She ran until her lungs screamed, then ran some more. She endured massages that were more like torture sessions to break up the scar tissue in her leg.

With Coach Temple's guidance, Wilma learned it wasn't just about how fast her legs could move, but *how* they moved. She studied the greats, mimicking their form, trying to unlock the smooth power that seemed to come effortlessly to others. Her stride was never going to be perfect, but it became undeniably hers – uneven, but filled with a fierce determination that transcended physical limitation.

Then came her first high school track meet. Wilma was so nervous she wanted to throw up. But when she heard the starting pistol, something shifted. The world narrowed to the lane in front of her, to the pounding of her heart and the sting of her breath, and she *ran*.

She didn't win.

In fact, she came dead last. But Coach Temple was oddly pleased. He saw something shift in Wilma that day, a realization that the competition wasn't just about crossing the finish line first, it was a battle with herself.

Wilma didn't rise to the top overnight. Those

early years were full of both triumph and disappointment. She won some races, then lost a whole series in a row. The voice of doubt would creep in – maybe the doctors were right, maybe this was as good as it would ever get.

But every time she fell, she got back up, a little wiser, a little stronger. Coach Temple became not just a coach, but a father figure, his gruff exterior hiding a deep well of belief both in her athletic potential and her strength as a person.

And then came Tennessee State University. Coach Temple secured her a spot, and there, Wilma truly began to blossom. She trained with relentless focus, pushing herself harder than ever before. But it wasn't just about the running anymore. University opened her eyes to a world beyond the limited confines of her small town. The Civil Rights Movement was in full swing, and on campus, she found a community of people fighting for the kind of equality she craved not just as an athlete, but as a Black woman in America.

She started winning races. A lot of races. Her uneven stride caught the attention of reporters, and they dubbed her "The Tennessee Gazelle" – a nickname both descriptive of her speed and a reminder that even the most graceful have their own imperfections. She didn't mind. It felt like a badge of honor, a testament to the battles she'd already overcome.

In 1956, Wilma qualified for the Olympics in Melbourne, Australia. It was surreal – the flight there, her first time on an airplane, let alone traveling across the world. She was a long way from the dusty yard where she'd chased after her brothers, but that fierce determination traveled with her.

The Melbourne Games weren't her shining moment athletically – she won bronze in the relay, a victory, but not the individual gold she hungered for. It was, however, an awakening. Here, athletes from all nationalities and backgrounds competed together, and in some small way, just by being there, she was helping chip away at the walls of division.

She returned home with a new fire in her belly. Four years till the next Olympics. Four years to train harder, to push further, to reach that seemingly impossible goal that flickered in her mind during those long, grueling training runs.

There's something magical about the Olympics. It's more than the athleticism, it's the weight of history, of dreams, and of people from every corner of the globe converging with a shared, almost childlike belief in the impossible. The 1960 Rome Olympics were even more special for Wilma. Italy, with its ancient ruins and air of timeless history, felt like a world away from the segregated South where she'd grown up.

But Wilma carried her own burdens onto the track. The pressure was immense, both from outside and the far harsher critic within herself. She'd dominated events leading up to the Games, raising expectations sky-high. There was the lingering feeling after Melbourne – was bronze the best she could do?

Then came the 100-meter dash. A hush fell over the stadium as Wilma took her place at the starting block. Years of struggle, of sweat and sacrifice and defying the odds, distilled into this single moment. The gun fired, and the world blurred.

She crossed the finish line and… silence. The timing machines seemed to take forever. Had she won? Had she choked under the pressure? Finally, the results flashed on the board. New world record. Olympic champion.

It wasn't just the athlete Wilma who stood on that podium, it was the little girl in braces, the young woman battling prejudice, and every person who'd ever been told they weren't good enough.

Her victories continued. The 200-meter dash – another gold. The 4x100 relay – gold again, shattering the world record with her teammates. The Fastest Woman in the World – and the title felt about more than just her speed.

Kerri Strug: Pain, Loyalty, and Gold

Kerri Strug wasn't built for gymnastics. Sure, she was strong, but she was also a little too tall, and not the willowy, flexible type usually dominating the sport. What she lacked in natural bendiness, she made up for with stubborn determination and a smile that could charm even the grumpiest Soviet judge.

Her parents, bless their hearts, enrolled her in gymnastics when she was a hyperactive toddler, hoping it would burn off some energy. Turns out, while Kerri was full of energy, it was a focused, competitive kind. She liked the structure, the challenge, and the thrill of hurtling her body through the air.

As a kid, Kerri was inseparable from her gymnastics bestie, Dominique Moceanu. Pint-sized powerhouses, they trained relentlessly, a blur of leotards and chalk dust. They were called "The Tiny Two," a mix of affection and a nod to how much younger they were than everyone else.

By the early 1990s, everyone knew their names. Kerri made the US National team, traveling to competitions worldwide where the stoic Russians were their biggest rivals. Gymnastics is weird – it's graceful, but also kinda brutal on your body. Kerri endured her fair share of injuries, but she bounced back (sometimes literally) with the kind of resilience that can't be taught.

The Olympics were the ultimate goal, the thing every gymnast dream of since their first wobbly cartwheel. Kerri qualified for the 1992 Barcelona Games, but at just fourteen, she was deemed a little too young to handle the pressure. She watched from the sidelines as her teammates competed, secretly vowing that next time would be different.

Fast forward to 1996. Olympic trials were crazy intense. These weren't cute kids anymore, these were athletes vying for a spot in history. Kerri, alongside Dominique and a crew of talented gymnasts, were dubbed the "Magnificent Seven." The hype was real, and America expected gymnastics gold for the first time as a unified team.

Their coach, Bela Karolyi, was a legend – and kind of terrifying. Imagine a gruff Eastern European who could spot a wobbly toe on a balance beam from across a crowded arena. He pushed them hard, too hard sometimes, but he also got results.

Training camp with Bela was no joke. Think endless repetitions, lectures about the importance of pointed toes, and the ever-present threat of extra conditioning if he wasn't satisfied. Kerri secretly called him "Count Dracula" due to his thick accent and slightly scary demeanor, but she grudgingly respected his methods.

What made the team special wasn't just their talent; it was their bond. They were teenagers thrown together under immense pressure, a weird mix of fierce rivals and inseparable friends. There were tears, laughter, secret snacks stashed from Bela, and more inside jokes than anyone could keep track of.

The Olympics loomed, and even with all their success, a tiny voice of doubt whispered in the back of Kerri's mind. The Russians were their old-school rivals: fierce, disciplined, and known for performing insanely difficult routines. The Americans were younger, flashier, with a dash of showmanship that Bela grudgingly tolerated. It was going to be a showdown.

The moment Kerri was carried off the podium, she went from athlete to icon. Her image was everywhere: newspapers, magazines, even Wheaties cereal boxes. America loves an underdog story, but this was next level. It was as if her single act of courage encapsulated the whole Olympic spirit.

The Atlanta Olympics were on home turf, which either means glory or crumbling under pressure. The Magnificent Seven performed spectacularly...until the final rotation. The vault. Power, precision, and the chance to clench the team gold.

Kerri prepared for her first vault. She sprinted down the runway, hit the springboard, and launched into the air. Disaster. She landed badly, the dreaded, knee-buckling, sound-of-crunching-bones kind of bad. Pain shot through her ankle. She knew instantly something was wrong.

The thing about team gymnastics is, there

are no timeouts. Her teammates had to nail their vaults without knowing if she could get back out there for her second attempt. The whole sport is built around individual perfection, but sometimes, grit looks a lot less glamorous.

Kerri limped away, team doctors swarming. They wrapped her ankle, face tight. Could she do it? Should she do it? The US was narrowly ahead of the Russians, but only if Kerri secured a decent score on her final vault. Otherwise, the dream was over.

Here's where things get both heroic and a touch controversial. Bela, being Bela, practically carried Kerri back to the vault runway. Her teammates stood there, nerves jangling, knowing what was at stake.

Kerri took off, hit the springboard, and somehow did the vault. The landing was another rough one. Agony ripped through her injured ankle – she basically hopped on one foot, then collapsed. The crowd gasped in a mix of horror and awe.

She didn't stick the landing like a champion, but in the world of gymnastics, it counted. Her score was just enough. The Magnificent

Seven had their gold medals, a wave of relief and exhilaration washing over the arena.

Bela, in an unprecedented display of emotion, swept Kerri off her feet for the iconic victory lap – a tiny gymnast carried by her intimidating coach, both of them grinning.

Overnight, Kerri had to navigate fame she'd never asked for. Interviews, talk shows, awkward encounters where people knew her but she had no clue who they were...all while trying to heal from a seriously injured ankle. There was also the question everyone asked: "Would you do it again?"

The debate raged. Some called it heroism, the ultimate team sacrifice. Others questioned whether it was necessary, whether Bela should have protected his athlete instead of pushing her to risk further damage. Gymnastics is a weird sport – one moment you're applauded for impossible feats, the next you're criticized for pushing your body too far.

Kerri herself was refreshingly down-to-earth about it all. In interviews, she emphasized it was a team decision, fueled by adrenaline and the single-minded focus of wanting that gold medal. She never regretted it, but also didn't want young gymnasts thinking they had to always sacrifice their bodies in the name of victory.

The injury healed, but surprisingly, Kerri was done with elite gymnastics. She went to college, living a semi-normal life while balancing the occasional Wheaties commercial. She became a teacher, married, had kids – proof that there's more to life than even Olympic glory.

But Kerri's legacy isn't just about that one vault. It's a reminder that true heroism doesn't always look glamorous. Sometimes, it's about showing up for your team, doing your best even when it's scary, and knowing when to ask for help when you need it.

Maybe she wasn't the most flexible gymnast, and the 1996 Olympics weren't a picture-perfect display of athletic dominance. But it was real, and gritty, and strangely inspiring.

Years later, some reporter asked Kerri if the pain was worth it. She grinned and said something along the lines of: "The gold medal is pretty cool, but honestly? The best part was the epic sleepover at the Olympic Village with my best friends."

That, right there, is what makes her story resonate, even decades later. It's about heart, friendship, and a moment of imperfect bravery that the world couldn't look away from.

Derek Redmond: A Track and Life Hero

Can you imagine running as fast as lightning? That's what Derek Redmond could do! Ever since he was a little boy, Derek seemed to float over the ground, his speed was so great.

Derek Redmond wasn't built like your typical 400-meter sprinter. He was tall, gangly even, not the muscle-bound powerhouse you'd expect to dominate a race. But Derek had other strengths – unwavering determination and a stubborn refusal to quit. Running was in his blood. His dad, Jim, was an avid runner, and Derek was basically born with sneakers on his feet.

By his teens, Derek was already a track star in his native Britain. He was fast, focused, and had a knack for breaking his own records – along with a few bones along the way. Injuries seem to love sprinters, and Derek had his fair share. Yet, he always bounced back, his Olympic dream keeping him motivated.

See, the Olympics isn't just about winning; it's about pushing yourself to the limit, testing your body and your spirit on the world's biggest stage. Derek wasn't the fastest out of the gate, but he was a finisher. He'd kick into high gear at the end of the race, surging past opponents who thought they'd already won. He wasn't just in it for the medals; he loved the challenge, the pure feeling of running at full tilt.

Fast forward to the 1992 Olympics in Barcelona. After a grueling series of qualifying races, Derek stood on the starting line in the semi-finals of the 400 meters. His dad, Jim, was in the stands, nerves jangling and camera at the ready. This was the moment they'd worked towards, sacrificed for, a lifetime of hopes and dreams condensed into less than one minute of pure adrenaline.

The starting gun fired. Derek burst out of the blocks, strong and steady. The first half of the race was a blur of pounding legs and roaring crowds. He was in good position, fighting his way to the front of the pack. And then...disaster. His hamstring snapped. It felt like a gunshot in the back of his leg. Agony shot through him, and he crumpled to the track.

The other sprinters streaked past. The dream was over. Medics rushed out, but Derek was in a world of his own pain and disappointment. His body had betrayed him at the worst possible moment. Years of work, shattered in seconds. The stretcher was ready to carry him off, a symbol of defeat. But that stubborn streak in Derek refused to give up.

With tears in his eyes, he pushed away the paramedics and stood, wobbling on one good leg. He wasn't about to be carried away. He had to finish the race. So, Derek began to hobble. It was a painful, awkward sight, each step a testament to raw grit more than athletic prowess.

The crowd started out confused, then hushed. Then, something incredible happened. They started to cheer. 80,000 people in the stadium, roaring for the guy in last place. Each agonizing hop was met with thunderous applause. Runners stopped mid-race, watching this display of heart over speed.

Suddenly, a figure emerged from the stands

and pushed through security. It was Jim, Derek's dad. Rules be damned, he wasn't about to let his son finish alone. He wrapped his arm around his son's waist, and together, father and son, they limped towards the finish line.

The crowd went wild. People were crying – even hardened sports reporters were getting a little misty-eyed. Derek crossed that line in last place, disqualified long ago, but in that moment, he was the biggest winner in the entire stadium.

The media went nuts. The story of the hobbling British runner became an Olympic sensation. It wasn't about speed, or perfect form, or even winning. It was about the human spirit, its astonishing ability to defy pain and disappointment. The Olympics are supposed to celebrate the world's best, but sometimes they showcase the world's bravest.

In the years that followed, Derek underwent multiple surgeries, but he never regained his top form as a sprinter. The physical damage was too severe. Yet, his story was far from over. He became a motivational speaker, sharing a message that resonated deeply with people, athletes and non-athletes alike.

Turns out, life is full of metaphorical hamstring snaps. Plans go sideways, dreams crumble, and we're left wondering why we even bother. Derek's message wasn't about always winning; it was about getting up when you fall, about finishing what you start even if it looks imperfect, about having the courage to defy expectations. Sometimes, the race that matters most is the one you run against yourself.

Derek faced criticism too. Some said he was attention-seeking, that he should have just accepted defeat gracefully. But his Olympic moment wasn't about ego; it was way more powerful than that. It was a visceral reminder that victory comes in many forms.

He went on to play other sports like basketball, and even did some TV commentary, becoming an all-around beloved sports figure. But those few minutes of hobbling in Barcelona are what he's best known for. And honestly? He's cool with that.

Turns out, Derek's most iconic race had little to do with perfect sprinting. He didn't break any speed records that day, but his determination and his dad's unwavering support broke through the hearts of millions. That image of father and son, crossing the finish line together, became a symbol of something far more important than medals: the unbreakable bond of family, and the relentless power of the human spirit to keep going, even when it hurts. And that kind of victory will always be worth its weight in gold.

Michael Phelps: Hyper to Hero

Little Michael Phelps had way too much energy. He bounced off walls, wiggled constantly, and even his teachers weren't sure if he had some kind of hyperactive disorder or was just built differently. His mom, Debbie, a school principal, wasn't about to let him run wild. She channeled that energy into sports – anything to tire him out a little.

Michael tried the usuals: baseball, soccer, a brief stint as a wrestler (hilarious in retrospect for anyone picturing his swimmer physique). Nothing quite clicked until he hit the pool. At first, swimming was less about Olympic dreams and more about the simple fact that he wasn't a danger to himself underwater.

But something shifted once he got the hang of it. Turns out, those long, lanky limbs and freakishly large wingspan were perfectly suited to slicing through water. Plus, Michael had an almost obsessive competitive streak. Hating to lose at ANYTHING propelled him more than any coach's pep-talk.

By age ten, he was crushing records left and right for his age group. This wasn't just splashing around anymore – coaches recognized raw talent, the drive to push himself beyond what seemed possible. He started working with Bob Bowman, a coach who was both demanding and saw the potential beneath the goofy-kid exterior.

Practice with Coach Bowman was legendary. Think endless laps, perfecting every tiny detail of technique, and workouts so intense other swimmers whispered about Michael being part-fish. There were days he wanted to quit, trade his goggles for a baseball glove, or just sleep for a week straight.

But here's the thing about Michael: that competitive fire burned too hot to give up. Plus, he'd started setting goals for himself, and not just the "win a local meet" kind. He wanted to break records, make history, do things no swimmer had ever done. Call it cockiness or crazy determination, it drove him forward.

By 15, he was the youngest male to make the US Olympic team since like the 1930s. The Sydney Olympics were a cool experience, but he got fifth in the 200m butterfly – no medals that time. It fueled his fire even more.

The next few years were a blur of training, meets, and a growing reputation. People called him "Shark Boy" – partly because of his focus in the water, partly because of his insane diet (rumors swirled about him eating enough calories to fuel a small army).

Then came the 2004 Athens Olympics. Michael won medal after medal, dominating events in a way that stunned the swimming world. But it was Beijing 2008 where he truly became a legend. Eight events. Eight gold medals. He broke world records that seemed unbreakable, some set by his hero, Mark Spitz, decades before.

The media exploded. His face was everywhere, with his slightly goofy grin and arms weighed down by enough gold to make a pirate jealous. It wasn't just the wins, it was how he won – by milliseconds, pushing himself and everyone else to redefine what they thought was possible in the sport.

The roar of the crowd in Beijing faded into an uncomfortable silence. The medals, once a symbol of relentless pursuit, now felt heavy around his neck. Michael Phelps had done it - achieved the impossible, rewritten the history books, and yet, a gnawing emptiness lingered within him.

For years, the pool had been his sanctuary. The rhythm of the strokes, the burn of his muscles, the singular goal of the finish line provided a kind of clarity that life on land never offered. He wasn't just Michael, the hyper kid or the awkward teen. He was the Shark, the record-breaker, the one to beat.

Suddenly, the structure was gone. With no world records left to conquer, no more Olympic titles to strive for, his carefully constructed identity began to crumble. The adrenaline rush of victory was replaced by a restless void that endless workouts couldn't fill.

The media spotlight, once thrilling, turned into a harsh glare. Every misstep, every ill-advised night out, was amplified and dissected for the world to see. The kid who couldn't sit still in class was now expected to be the poster boy of perfection, the invincible champion. The pressure was immense, and without the guiding force of his Olympic dream, he faltered.

There was the infamous leaked photo that tarnished his golden image. The driving infraction arrest, the public apologies that felt hollow even as he uttered them. The whispers of disappointment grew louder. It was a stark reminder that even superheroes don't get a free pass, that the weight of expectation can crush even the strongest shoulders.

Michael Phelps was lost. The thing that had defined him for so long was gone, and he wasn't sure who he was without it. Retirement, instead of a triumphant finish line, felt like a disorienting fall into the unknown.

But there's a strange resilience in champions, even when they stumble. Michael sought help, confronting the demons he'd masked with single-minded focus for years. It was slow and painful, an internal battle far harder than any swim meet. He reconnected with his family, with old friends from the days before Olympic mania. He learned that vulnerability wasn't weakness, but a different kind of strength altogether.

The road to the 2012 London Olympics was driven by something more than just the hunger for more medals. It was about proving to himself, more than anyone else, that he was still capable of facing challenges, overcoming setbacks, and rising again.

The swimming was still phenomenal, but there was a maturity about him now. When he wasn't in the pool, he was seen mentoring younger teammates, the cocky kid replaced with a leader ready to pass the torch. When the inevitable questions about his past mistakes surfaced, he answered with honesty tinged with regret, a willingness to own his flaws.

The Rio Olympics in 2016 became his final, triumphant act. The roar of the crowd now held a note of bittersweet nostalgia. The gold medals were still sweet, but they were also a reminder of the journey, of the boy who'd used the pool to tame his restless energy and the man who'd fought his way back to the top after stumbles along the way.

The medals will always be part of the Michael Phelps legend. But his true legacy lies in the human side of his story.

Abebe Bikila: Barefoot to Legend

Abebe Bikila wasn't your typical Olympic hopeful. Far from the world of celebrity athletes and rigorous training camps, he served in the Ethiopian Imperial Guard. While the title held a certain air of grandeur, the reality was long hours and routine duties. But within Abebe, a different kind of fire burned – a passion for running that transcended the confines of his military service.

His training sessions were far from glamorous. Forget climate-controlled gyms and meticulously measured treadmills. Abebe ran long distances, his feet pounding the dusty Ethiopian terrain. It wasn't just a casual jog; it was a relentless pursuit of personal limits, a testament to his raw talent and unwavering determination. It was during these solitary runs that Abebe caught the eye of a perceptive coach, who recognized the potential simmering beneath the surface.

The 1960 Rome Olympics loomed on the

horizon, and the coach saw an opportunity for Abebe to showcase his extraordinary abilities. There was just one small obstacle – Abebe lacked proper running shoes. His old ones were worn-out and flimsy, and the new issue from the team caused painful blisters. In a decision that would redefine his legacy, Abebe made a bold choice – he would run barefoot.

This was a time when Olympic events were a spectacle of uniformity, a stage where athletes adhered to specific standards. Abebe's barefoot defiance was met with a mixture of amusement and skepticism. Was he foolishly disregarding the importance of proper footwear? Or was there a hidden genius to his unorthodox approach? In the world of elite athletics, the line between eccentricity and innovation can be remarkably thin.

The marathon itself is a unique test of human endurance. 26.2 miles of relentless forward motion push even the most seasoned athletes to their physical and mental limits. The scorching Roman sun beat down on the unforgiving cobblestone streets, making the race an even more formidable challenge. The other competitors, clad in their high-tech running shoes, cast curious glances at Abebe, the barefoot soldier who seemed out of place amidst established running stars.

Yet, Abebe ran. His stride was smooth and efficient, his pace seemingly effortless. The lack of shoes, a source of initial bewilderment, became a point of fascination as he effortlessly navigated the course. The crowd, initially bemused, found themselves captivated by his unconventional approach. The cheers grew louder as the unexpected challenger started to dominate the race.

The final leg of the marathon took place under the illumination of flickering torches, an unusual occurrence for the time. With each powerful stride, Abebe left his competitors further behind. As he emerged from the torchlit path and entered the Olympic Stadium, a hush fell over the crowd. It was a moment of anticipation, a collective recognition that something extraordinary was about to unfold. Then, Abebe crossed the finish line, a full two minutes ahead of his nearest competitor. The silence erupted into a thunderous roar.

The world was stunned. Who was this unheralded Ethiopian runner with the unshakeable determination and the audacity to race barefoot? He had shattered the marathon world record on his first attempt, proving that success wasn't defined by fancy equipment, but by unwavering dedication and sheer physical prowess. He had not only become the first Black African Olympic gold medalist, but also redefined the very concept of athletic potential.

The media descended upon Abebe, christening him the "Barefoot Wonder." Shoe companies lined up with lucrative endorsement deals, hoping to capitalize on his unconventional victory. But Abebe remained grounded. While not averse to free running shoes, he understood that his triumph stemmed from his own unwavering spirit, not the brand he wore on his feet.

Four years later, the Olympic torch once again flickered, marking the start of the Tokyo Games. Abebe returned to the world stage, older and seasoned with fame, but with the same unwavering passion for running. This time, however, he sported shoes, a concession to the persistent questions about whether his barefoot victory was a fluke. Additionally, he had battled appendicitis in the years following his Rome triumph, throwing a wrench into his usual rigorous training regime.

The media narrative had shifted. Doubts lingered about his ability to repeat his historic feat. Could the barefoot wonder from Rome compete with the new generation of running stars who had emerged since his victory? Abebe, however, remained unfazed. He possessed an inner calm that belied his competitive fire.

The starting gun echoed through the stadium, and Abebe surged forward, taking the lead from the outset. This time, there were no barefoot theatrics, but a controlled determination that spoke volumes about his mental fortitude and physical resilience.

As he crossed the finish line, the roar of the crowd confirmed what many had suspected all along – Abebe Bikila was not a one-hit wonder. He had shattered his own Olympic record, proving that his Rome victory was no fluke, but a testament to his exceptional talent and unwavering spirit.

Abebe had not only cemented his place in Olympic history but also inspired countless individuals, particularly those from marginalized communities, to pursue their dreams with unwavering determination. His story was a powerful reminder that success is not defined by external factors or preconceived notions, but by the strength of one's will and the unwavering belief in one's own potential.

Abebe's legacy extended far beyond the realm of athletics. He became a symbol of national pride for Ethiopia, a beacon of hope for those facing adversity, and an embodiment of the human spirit's ability to overcome seemingly insurmountable challenges. His story transcended cultural and geographical boundaries, resonating with individuals from all walks of life who found inspiration in his unwavering determination and unwavering belief in himself.

Abebe Bikila's legacy is one of courage, perseverance, and the unwavering pursuit of excellence. He demonstrated that with unwavering determination and an unwavering belief in one's potential, even the most extraordinary achievements are within reach. His story serves as a timeless reminder that true greatness lies not in the absence of challenges, but in the ability to rise above them.

Abebe Bikila's legacy lives on, inspiring generations to embrace their dreams, challenge limitations, and push the boundaries of what is considered possible. His story is a testament to the indomitable human spirit, a reminder that even in the face of adversity, greatness can be achieved through unwavering determination and an unwavering belief in oneself.

Surya Bonaly: Defying Gravity

It's the 1998 Winter Olympics. The ice rink gleams, the crowd buzzes with anticipation, and a powerful, petite figure takes center stage. Music begins, but instead of the graceful twirls and jumps common in figure skating, she launches into a backflip – a move so daring it's technically illegal. The judges gasp, the audience roars... this is Surya Bonaly, the electrifying skater who brought a rebellious spirit to the ice.

But Surya's story began way before that iconic moment. Born in Nice, France, she wasn't your typical princess-in-tights kind of girl. Believe it or not, baby Surya was adopted from an orphanage! Her new parents, though, saw her spark and encouraged her wild energy. Gymnastics, trampoline, you name it – Surya was a fearless acrobat from the start.

So, how'd she end up on ice? Some folks say it was her coach, who saw potential in her explosive jumps. Others swear destiny was at work when young Surya's mom took her to see an ice show - that's when she fell in love with the power and freedom of skating.

Yet, even as she mastered those triple axels, Surya remained a rebel at heart. She was criticized by traditionalists who wanted frills, not flips. Skating was about elegance, they said. Surya, with her athletic style and fierce determination, showed them elegance could be powerful too.

Surya became a force to be reckoned with. European Championship titles? Check. World Championship medals? Check, check, and check! She was the first woman to try a quadruple jump in competition. A total badass, right? Well, the judges didn't always agree.

See, Surya had this thing about rules...she respected them, but she also wanted the freedom to be herself on the ice. They'd score her lower, even when she landed crazy-hard jumps perfectly. They said she lacked artistry. But here's the thing, Surya's artistry wasn't about twirling around like a ballerina, it was about raw power and fearless innovation.

Then came the 1994 World Championships.

Surya had skated her heart out, giving her absolute best. Yet, she ended up with silver. Frustrated and hurt, Surya made a decision that shocked the world. During the medal ceremony, she took off her silver medal and stood, defiantly, on the podium. The crowd was divided – some gasped, others cheered. Whatever the reaction, Surya sent a loud and clear message: she would not be defined by scores alone.

Some called her a sore loser, others hailed her as a champion of individuality. But for Surya, it wasn't about disrespect; it was about something far more important – demanding respect for her own style. Like, hey, just because she wasn't skating to Swan Lake didn't make her any less of an athlete an artist!

Surya's skating career had its ups and downs, but she never stopped pushing the boundaries. And that brings us back to the 1998 Olympics. It was her last competitive skate before turning professional, and true to form, Surya wasn't going out quietly.

In her final program, she knew the backflip was a long shot - banned in competition, and ridiculously hard to pull off on ice. But she also knew she'd regret not going for it. So, when the music reached its crescendo, Surya launched herself in the air. She landed the backflip on ONE BLADE! It wasn't perfect, but it was spectacular, a testament to her sheer guts.

The judges? Well, they docked points, of course. But the crowd went absolutely wild. Surya may not have medaled that day, but her performance went down in Olympic history as an act of daring and a refusal to play by everyone else's rules.

Surya Bonaly's legacy isn't just about her titles. Sure, she was an incredible athlete, but more importantly, she showed the world that you could be strong AND graceful, different AND exceptional. Her backflip became a symbol of defying expectations. It was a reminder – sometimes the most beautiful artistry lies in boldly being yourself.

After retiring from competition, Surya continued to shine. She toured with Champions on Ice, became a commentator, and settled in the US, coaching and inspiring new generations of skaters. She's even turned vegan and become an advocate for animal rights!

Because, true to her nature, Surya remains someone who stands up for what she believes in.

Dick Fosbury's Revolutionary Jump

Dick Fosbury was no athletic superstar. In fact, as a high schooler in Oregon, he was kind of clumsy. Coaches shook their heads as he ran at the high jump bar, because the kid couldn't seem to get the timing or coordination right on any of the traditional jumping styles. The straddle jump? A tangled mess. The Western Roll? A graceless belly flop.

But Dick had a stubborn streak. Most kids would have given up, but he was determined to clear that darn bar. And in that determination, he started messing around in his backyard. What if he jumped backward? What if he used the natural curve of his back to help get over the bar? Now, this was the 1960s, and sports weren't exactly a hotbed of creative thinking. Everyone jumped facing the bar, because that's just how it was done.

Dick, clearly, hadn't gotten the memo.

At first, it was comically bad. He couldn't get

any height and kept landing on his head with a painful-sounding *thud*. Imagine a flopping fish thrown out of water – that was Dick Fosbury. Neighbors probably peeked through their curtains, half amused, half worried the kid was seriously going to injure himself.

But Dick kept trying. Bit by bit, he adjusted his technique. Instead of running straight at the bar, he added a curve to his approach. He learned to arch his back and throw his legs skyward, clearing the bar like a very ungainly grasshopper. Sure, he looked utterly ridiculous, but a funny thing was happening – he was actually starting to go OVER the bar.

News of Dick's weird jumping style started to spread. Other high jumpers scoffed; this had to be a joke, right? Imagine their surprise when, against all odds, this goofy-jumping kid made it to the 1968 Olympic Games in Mexico City.

And here's Dick, about to debut his bizarre backwards technique in front of the whole world. The other athletes probably expected him to make a fool of himself.

But Dick Fosbury, clumsy and determined, was ready to shock them all.

The bar went higher and higher. Competitors using those old-fashioned styles started dropping out. Dick, however, kept sailing over, landing on the padded mat with a grin on his face. The jump wasn't pretty; journalists joked it looked like he'd been "shot out of a cannon, backwards." But Dick wasn't going for style points, he was going for results.

Suddenly, everyone was watching the lanky kid who wouldn't do things the "right" way. Could this backwards flop actually work? Dick answered that question with flying colors (or rather, flying backwards). Not only did he clear the bar, but he smashed the Olympic record and took home the gold medal. Dick Fosbury, the kid who couldn't jump to save his life, was now an Olympic champion.

The sports world went a little nuts. Headlines called it "The Flop Heard 'Round the World." Suddenly, kids all over were trying to jump like Dick, even though they probably landed on their butts more often than not. Dick faced a lot of critics. Some traditionalists called it unsafe or said it just wasn't how things were done. But something undeniable had happened – Dick had just changed the game.

Within just a few years, almost every high jumper on the planet had switched to the Fosbury Flop. Why? It's simple - when it came to getting over the bar, Dick's weird way just worked better. The higher the bar was raised, the more evident it became that this goofy backwards jump was the way of the future. Sometimes, it's the weirdos, the ones willing to experiment and question tradition, who end up making the greatest leaps.

Here's the coolest part: the Fosbury Flop is still the way high jumpers compete today! Even after all these years, no one has come up with a better way to fly over that bar. That's what true innovation is – when a new idea comes along and completely changes the way things are done.

Sarah Attar: Breaking Barriers

Sarah Attar was a track star unlike any other. Yes, she loved the rhythm of her stride, the way running made her feel strong and focused. But she also had an artist's soul, forever noticing the subtle dance of light and shadow on landscapes, drawn to nature's quiet beauty. She expressed herself through photography, capturing the world with a unique perspective.

Growing up in sunny California with dual Saudi Arabian and American citizenship, Sarah was a blend of two worlds. In California, women's sports were celebrated, track stars were role models, and pushing boundaries was encouraged. But her father's heritage, his stories of Saudi Arabia, echoed with a different reality – a place where women in sports faced deeply ingrained obstacles.

Track and field, especially long-distance events, weren't a familiar path for girls in Saudi Arabia. In fact, before 2012, no Saudi woman had ever competed in the

Olympics. The reasons were complex—a mix of strict traditions, religious interpretations, and limited facilities and opportunities for women in sports. Sarah, with her quiet determination, wasn't content to accept those limitations.

Opportunity knocked in 2008. Sarah, with her natural talent and drive, was recruited for Pepperdine University's track and field team. She flourished, her artistry finding expression in the disciplined beauty of running. Yet, a question lingered. Could she, a dual citizen, find a way to represent her father's homeland, Saudi Arabia, on the grandest athletic stage, the Olympics?

The road to the 2012 London Olympics wasn't a smooth track for Sarah. The Saudi Arabian Olympic Committee traditionally didn't allow female athletes to participate. Yet, the tides were starting to turn. The International Olympic Committee was pushing for greater representation, making it clear that nations excluding women would face consequences.

The news came like a jolt of electricity: Sarah Attar, along with another athlete, would become the first-ever women to represent

Saudi Arabia in the Olympics. It was historic, groundbreaking...and polarizing. Critics were vocal, claiming it was disrespectful of Saudi Arabian traditions. Others worried she'd be at a physical disadvantage, forced to compete in a full-body running suit and headscarf instead of the standard, streamlined uniforms. Sarah remained focused, embracing the challenge. This outfit held deep cultural significance, and she was determined to show that athleticism and modesty could coexist.

The 800 meters, her chosen event, was a brutal sprint, a test of speed and stamina. Sarah trained relentlessly, knowing the world's eyes would be on her. It wouldn't just be about athletic prowess; every stride she took was a stride against deeply ingrained stereotypes and societal limitations.

The day of the race arrived, the London stadium buzzing with energy. As Sarah stepped onto the track, history hung in the air. This wasn't just about running a race; it was about rewriting the narrative for women across a nation and challenging the world's perceptions.

The starting gun fired, and Sarah surged

forward. The other runners, in their sleek outfits and with years of unfettered training, quickly pulled ahead. Some might have seen this as disappointing, a symbol of how far Saudi female athletes had to go. But Sarah's eyes held a fierce determination. She didn't just represent herself; she carried the hopes of countless girls and women who dared to dream bigger.

The crowd roared, recognizing the significance of the moment. Every stride Sarah took challenged decades of misconceptions. She proved that a woman could be strong in her faith, honor her traditions, and still be a fierce competitor on a global stage. This wasn't just an 800-meter race; it was a declaration.

While Sarah's final time was far from a medal, her impact was immeasurable. As she crossed the finish line, the loudest cheers weren't about her placement, but about the moment she created. Images of a woman in a headscarf, running with unwavering determination, were beamed around the world. Sarah Attar, runner and artist, had painted a powerful portrait of resilience, shattering stereotypes with every step.

Her Olympic debut wasn't the finish line, but the start of something bigger. It was a declaration that women, regardless of where they come from, what they wear, or the traditions they uphold, deserve a chance to chase their dreams. And sometimes, the greatest victories are those that echo long after the final lap.

Billy Mills: From the Reservation to Olympic Glory

Imagine a vast, grassy landscape under a big South Dakota sky. That's where Billy Mills was born, a kid with Oglala Lakota Sioux heritage, growing up on the Pine Ridge Indian Reservation in 1938. Life was far from easy. Poverty, prejudice, and the lingering pain of past injustices were a constant hum in the background of his childhood. To top it off, he lost his mother at the young age of 12. Heartbreak could've easily crushed him.

But Billy had a spark inside. It wasn't about fancy sneakers or perfect technique – the kid just loved to run. It wasn't just the physical challenge; running was his escape, a way to feel strong and powerful in a world that often told him he wasn't. He'd race for miles across the open plains, his bare feet hardly making a sound.

High school changed things. Sure, he was small and wiry, not your typical athletic build, but Billy was fast. Like, insanely fast. He smashed school records left and right, turning heads even beyond his reservation. And it wasn't just about competition - running felt like a way to honor something deep inside of him, a connection to his ancestors who also roamed these lands with endurance and spirit. With his newfound recognition, Billy earned an athletic scholarship to the University of Kansas. A ticket to a wider world, and a chance to show everyone what he could do.

Kansas was a whole new ball game. Billy was miles away from home, a Native American kid on a big campus with unfamiliar faces. There were times when racism and doubt stung. But on the track, under the guidance of his supportive coach, Billy found his place. He joined the cross-country team and became a force no one could ignore, racking up win after win with his fierce determination.

While all this was happening, Billy's life took an even sweeter turn - he fell in love and married his sweetheart, Pat. She believed in him as much as he did, pushing him to be his best, on and off the track. He also found purpose by joining the U.S. Marine Corps as an officer, serving his country while never giving up on his Olympic dreams.

Now, 1964 rolls around, and guess who makes an almost impossible cut? Billy qualifies for the Tokyo Olympics in the 10,000-meter race. Honestly, the odds were against him. He was the underdog, the guy no one really expected to do much against experienced favorites. But Billy? He was just happy to have a shot, to live the dream he'd carried since those early days running through the open fields.

Race day. The Olympic stadium buzzes with anticipation. Billy lines up, a quiet focus in his eyes. As the gun fires, the favorites surge forward, and Billy...kind of hangs back. The commentators are probably scratching their heads, wondering why this guy even bothered to show up. But lap after lap, something incredible starts to happen.

It's like Coach Riley's words echoed in Billy's ears - he once told him to use his determination, to find the wings of an eagle when he needed strength. And find them, he did. Billy starts to pick up speed, passing runners with stunning force. The crowd gasps - is this unknown American actually making a comeback?

The final lap is pure adrenaline. The favorites are duking it out, jockeying for position, but Billy bursts past them with a surge of unexpected power, as if every ancestor, every doubt, every bit of hardship he's ever faced is propelling him forward. His legs churn, arms pump, and he crosses the finish line first.

Olympic gold. A new record. And look, there are literal jaws dropping in the stands. Billy Mills, the kid from the reservation, the underdog no one saw coming, just defied every expectation. They had to play the American national anthem for a guy many in his own country wouldn't have shared a bus seat with back then. Talk about a statement.

Billy went on to inspire millions. He became a voice for Native American youth, reminding them that they too can defy the odds, that sometimes the best victories are won against your own doubts. He founded 'Running Strong for American Indian Youth,' proving that sometimes, it's not just about the medal, but what you do with your victory to lift up those behind you.

US Hockey Team: Against All Odds

Alright, hockey fans, get ready for the most epic underdog story in sports history – the "Miracle on Ice!" Here's a look at how a bunch of ragtag American college kids shocked the world:

Okay, the year is 1980. Picture big hair, bad pop music, and the Cold War simmering between the USA and the Soviet Union (that's Russia back in the day). This wasn't just political tension; it seeped into everything, even sports. And when it came to hockey...well, the Soviets were basically unbeatable.

Think of them as the final boss in a video game – they had a team of seasoned pros who trained together year-round. They won four straight Olympic gold medals, crushing everyone in their path, proving communist superiority with every slap shot (or so they thought).

Meanwhile, the US hockey team? A bunch of college kids. Sure, they were talented, but young and scrappy, the definition of the underdog. They were thrown together by coach Herb Brooks, a guy with an intense style and a weird love for making players skate until they puked. The team didn't exactly get along at first – you had guys from Boston who hated guys from Minnesota, rivalries running deep. But Coach Brooks was determined to mold them into something special.

The 1980 Winter Olympics were in Lake Placid, New York. A small town, a big stage, and the USA was barely considered a serious contender. In the rounds leading to the medal games, the Soviets steamrolled their opponents. Like, 10-3 victories, 17-4...total domination. The US? They squeaked by with some wins, a few lucky ties. Everyone figured their Cinderella story was about to end with a very harsh Soviet reality check.

Cut to the day of the big semi-final showdown. The atmosphere's electric. If the USA loses this, they're out, no shot at the gold. The Soviets take the ice, looking intimidating with their iconic red uniforms and their reputation for being ice-cold hockey machines. The crowd figures, well, it was fun while it lasted, America.

But here's the thing about underdogs: they have nothing to lose, and that can make them dangerous. Coach Brooks gives a fiery locker room speech, reminding his team that they might be young, but they've got heart. And hey, a little bit of crazy belief in the impossible doesn't hurt either.

The puck drops. The first period isn't pretty. The Soviets score, just like everyone expected. The Americans struggle to keep up, but goalie Jim Craig is playing out of his mind, making insane saves. Then something unexpected happens – the US scores! The crowd goes nuts. But the Soviets strike back, ending the period ahead 2-1.

Second period, the Americans refuse to back down. They fight tooth and nail for every inch of ice, scrappy and determined. The crowd's on their feet, sensing that maybe, just maybe, there's a flicker of hope. Against all odds, the US ties the game at 2-2. Now, it's getting real interesting.

The final period...talk about nail-biting. The lead switches back and forth, the Soviets score, then America's captain Mike Eruzione pops one in to tie it up. Ten minutes left. Five minutes. The tension is unbearable. Could the unthinkable happen?

Then, with just seconds on the clock...Eruzione does it again! He fires a shot that rockets past the Soviet goalie. The crowd erupts – you'd think the roof was gonna come off! The final buzzer sounds: USA 4, SOVIETS 3. A bunch of American college kids just beat the unbeatable.

The US team storms the ice, piling on top of each other in a tangle of joy and disbelief. In the stands, the chant starts, echoing through the stadium, across the country, around the world: "USA! USA! USA!" This wasn't just a hockey game anymore; it was a symbol of hope, grit, and a whole lot of American pride in a time when people desperately needed something to cheer for.

But the story's not over! Remember, this was only the semi-finals. The US still had to face Finland for the gold. Galvanized by their win, they didn't let up. They beat Finland 4-2, clinching the most unlikely Olympic victory imaginable.

News of the "Miracle on Ice" spread like wildfire. These college kids weren't just hockey players anymore; they were heroes, proving that even the longest of long shots can sometimes, miraculously, hit the net. They inspired a nation and showed the world that with determination, heart, and a belief in the impossible, anything is possible.

Thank you so much for

making this so far

We invite you to leave a quick review! It will only take a few seconds and can be as brief as a couple of words.

To leave your feedback:

1. Open your camera app
2. Point your mobile device at the QR code below
3. The review page will appear in your web browser

Made in the USA
Monee, IL
03 July 2024

61180689R10075